NATIVE

EASTERN MIWOK TRIBE

by
Mary Null Boulé

Illustrated by
Daniel Liddell

Merryant Publishers, Inc.
Vashon, WA 98070
206-463-3879

Book Number Twelve in a series of twenty-six

This series is dedicated to Virginia Harding, whose editing expertise and friendship brought this project to fruition.

J
970.3
B664em

Library of Congress Catalog Card Number: 92-61897

ISBN: 1-877599-36-0

Copyright © 1992, Merryant Publishing

7615 S.W. 257th St., Vashon, WA 98070.

No part of this book may be reproduced without permission in writing from the publisher.

FOREWORD

Native American people of the United States are often living their lives away from major cities and away from what we call the mainstream of life. It is, then, interesting to learn of the important part these remote tribal members play in our everyday lives.

More than 60% of our foods come from the ancient Native American's diet. Farming methods of today also can be traced back to how tribal women grew crops of corn and grain. Many of our present day ideas of democracy have been taken from tribal governments. Even some 1,500 Native American words are found in our English language today.

Fur traders bought furs from tribal hunters for small amounts of money, sold them to Europeans and Asians for a great deal of money, and became rich. Using their money to buy land and to build office buildings, some traders started business corporations which are now the base of our country's economy.

There has never been enough credit given to these early Americans who took such good care of our country when it was still in their care. The time has come to realize tribal contributions to our society today and to give Native Americans not only the credit, but the respect due them.

Mary Boulé

A-frame cradle for girls; tule matting. Tubatulabal tribe.

GENERAL INFORMATION

Creation legends told by today's tribal people speak of how, very long ago, their creator placed them in a territory, where they became caretakers of that land and its animals. None of their ancient legends tells about the first Native Americans coming from another continent.

It is important to respect the different beliefs and theories, to learn from and seek the truth in all of them.

Villagers' tribal history lessons do not agree with the beliefs of anthropologists (scientific historians who study the habits and customs of humans).

Clues found by these scientists lead them to believe that ancient tribespeople came to North America from Asia during the Ice Age period some 20 to 35 thousand years ago. They feel these humans walked over a land strip in the Bering Straits, following animal herds who provided them with food.

Scientists' understanding of ancient people must come from studying clues; for example, tools, utensils, baskets, garbage discoveries, and stories they passed from one generation to the next.

California's Native Americans did not organize into large tribes. Instead they divided into tribelets, sometimes having as many as 250 people. Some tribelets had only one chief for each village.

From 20 to 100 people could be living in one village, which usually had several houses. In most cases, these groups of people were one family and were related to each other. From five to ten people of a family might live in one house. For instance, a mother, a father, two or three children, a grandmother, or aunt or daughter-in-law might live together.

Village members together would own the land important to them for their well-being. Their land might include oak trees with precious acorns, streams and rivers, and plants which were good to eat. Streams and rivers were especially important to a tribe's quality of life. Water drew animals to it; that meant more food for the tribe to eat. Fish were a good source of food, and traveling by boat was often easier than walking long distances. Water was needed in every part of tribal life.

Village and tribelet land was carefully guarded. Each group knew exactly where the boundaries of its land were found. Boundaries were known by landmarks such as mountains or rivers, or they might also be marked by poles planted in the ground. Some boundary lines were marked by rocks, or by objects placed there by tribal members. The size of a territory had to be large enough to supply food to every person living there.

The California tribes spoke many languages. Sometimes villages close together even had a problem understanding one another. This meant that each group had to be sure of the boundaries of other tribes around them when gathering food. It would not be wise to go against the boundaries and the customs of neighbors. The Native Americans found if they respected the boundaries of their neighbors, not so many wars had to be fought. California tribes, in spite of all their differences, were not as warlike as other tribes in our country.

Not only did the California tribes speak different languages, but their members also differed in size. Some tribes were very tall, almost six feet tall. The shortest people came from the Yuki tribe which had territory in what is now Mendocino County. They measured only about 5'2" tall. All Native Americans, regardless of size, had strong, straight black hair and dark brown eyes.

TRADE

Trading between tribes was an important part of life. Inland tribes had large animal hides that coastal tribes wanted. By trading the hides to coastal groups, inland tribes would receive fish and shells, which they in turn wanted. Coastal tribes also wanted minerals and rocks mined in the mountains by inland tribes. Obsidian rock from the northern mountains was especially wanted for arrowheads. There were, as well, several minerals, mined in the inland mountains, which could be made into the colorful body paints needed for religious ceremonies.

Southern tribes particularly wanted steatite from the Gabrielino tribe. Steatite, or soapstone, was a special metal which allowed heat to spread evenly through it. This made it a good choice to be used for cooking pots and flat frying pans. It could be carved into bowls because of its softness and could be decorated by carving designs into it. Steatite came from Catalina Island in the Coastal Gabrielino territory. Gabrielinos found steatite to be a fine trading item to offer for the acorns, deerskins, or obsidian stone they needed.

When people had no items to trade but needed something, they used small strings of shells for money. The small dentalium shells, which came from the far distant Northwest coast, had great value. Strings of dentalia usually served as money in the Northern California tribes, although some dentalia was used in the Central California tribes.

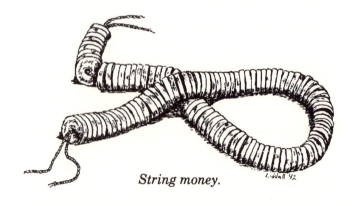

String money.

In southern California clam shells were broken and holes were bored through the center of each piece. Then the pieces were rounded and polished with sandstone and strung into strings for money. These were not thought to be as valuable as dentalia.

Strings of shell money were measured by tattoo marks on the trader's lower arm or hand.

Here is a sample of shell value:

> A house, three strings
> A fishing place, one to three strings
> Land with acorn-bearing oak trees, one to five strings

A great deal of rock and stone was traded among the tribes for making tools. Arrows had to have sharp-edged stone for tips. The best stone for arrow tips was obsidian (volcanic glass) because, when hit properly, it broke off into flakes with very sharp edges. California tribes considered obsidian to be the most valuable rock for trading.

Some tribes had craftsmen who made knives with wooden handles and obsidian blades. Often the handles were decorated with carvings. Such knives were good for trading purposes. Stone mortars and pestles, used by the women for grinding grains into flour, were good trading items.

BASKETS & POTTERY

California tribal women made beautiful baskets. The Pomo and Chumash baskets, what few are left, show us that the women of those tribes might have been some of the finest basketmakers in the world. Baskets were used for gathering and storing food, for carrying babies, and even for hauling water. In emergencies, such as flooding waters, sometimes children, women, and tribal belongings crossed the swollen rivers and streams in huge, woven baskets! Baskets were so tightly woven that not a drop of water could leak from them.

Baskets also made fine cooking pots. Very hot rocks were taken from a fire and tossed around inside baskets with a looped tree branch until food in the basket was cooked.

Most baskets were made to do a certain job, but some baskets were designed for their beauty alone and were excellent for trading. Older women of a tribe would teach young girls how to weave baskets.

Pottery was not used by many California tribes. What little there was seems to have been made by those tribes living near to the Navaho and Mohave tribes of Arizona, and it shows their style. For example, pottery of the California tribes did not have much decoration and was usually a dull red color. Designs were few and always in yellow.

Ohlone hunter wearing deerskin camouflage.

Long thin coils of clay were laid one on top the other. Then the coils were smoothed between a wooden paddle and a small stone to shape the bowl. Pottery from California Native Americans has been described as light weight and brittle (easily broken), probably because of the kind of clay soil found in California.

HUNTING & FISHING

Tribal men spent much of their time making hunting and fishing tools. Bows and arrows were built with great care, to make them shoot as accurately as possible. Carelessly made hunting weapons caused fewer animals to be killed and people then had less food to eat.

Bows made by men of Southern California tribes were made long and narrow. In the northern part of the state bows were a little shorter, thinner, and wider than those of their northern neighbors. Size and thickness of bows depended on the size trees growing in a tribe's territory. The strongest bows were wrapped with sinew, the name given to animal tendons. Sinew is strong and elastic like a rubber band.

Arrows were made in many sizes and shapes, depending on their use. For hunting larger animals, a two-piece arrow was used. The front piece of the arrow shaft was made so that it would remain in the animal, even if the back part was removed or broken off. The arrowhead, or point, was wrapped to the front piece of the shaft. This kind of arrow was also used in wars.

Young boys used a simple wooden arrow with the end sharpened to a point. With this they could hunt small animals like birds and rabbits. The older men of the tribe taught boys how to make their own arrows, how to aim properly, and how to repair broken weapons.

Tribal men spent many hours making and mending fishing nets. The string used in making nets often came from the fibers of plants. These fibers were twisted to make them strong and tough, then knotted into netting. Fences, or weirs, that had one small opening for fish, were built across streams. As the fish swam through the opening they would be caught in netting or harpooned by a waiting fisherman.

Hooks, if used at all, were cut from shells. Mostly hooks could be found when the men fished in large lakes or when catching trout in high mountain areas. Hooks were attached to heavy plant fiber string.

Dip nets, made of netting attached to branches that were bent into a circle, were used to catch fish swimming near shore. Dip nets had long handles so the fishermen could reach deep into the water.

Sometimes a mild poison was placed on the surface of shallow water. This confused the fish and caused them to float to the surface of the water, where they could be scooped up by a waiting fisherman. Not enough poison was used to make humans ill.

Not all fishing was done from the shore. California tribes used two kinds of boats when fishing. Canoes, dug out of one half a log, were useful for river fishing. These were square at each end, round on the bottom, and very heavy. Some of them were well-finished, often even having a carved seat in them.

Today we think of "balsa" as a very lightweight wood, but in Spanish, the word balsa means "raft". That is why Spanish explorers called the Native American canoes, made from tule reeds, "balsa" boats.

Balsa boats were made of bundled tule reeds and were used throughout most of California. They made into safe, lightweight boats for lake and river use. Usually the balsa canoe had a long, tightly tied bundle of tule for the boat bottom and one bundle for each side of the canoe. The front of the canoe was higher than the back. Balsa boats could be steered with a pole or with a paddle, like a raft.

Men did most of the fishing, women were in charge of gathering grasses, seeds, and acorns for food. After the food was collected, it was either eaten right away or made ready for winter storage.

Except for a few southern groups, California tribes had permanent villages where they lived most of the year. They also had food-gathering places they returned to each year to collect acorns, salt, fish, and other foods not found near their villages.

FOOD

Many different kinds of plant food grew wild in California in the days before white people arrived. Berries and other plant foods grew in the mountains. Forests offered the local tribes everything from pine nuts to animals.

Native Americans found streams full of fish for much of the year. Inland fresh water lakes had large tule reeds growing along their shores. Tule could be eaten as food when plants were young and tender. More important, however, tule was used in making fabric for clothes and for building boats and houses. Tule was probably the most useful plant the California Native Americans found growing wild in their land.

Like all deserts, the one in southern California had little water or fish, but small animals and cactus plants made good food for the local tribes. They moved from place to place harvesting whatever was ripe. Tribal members always knew when and where to find the best food in their territory.

Acorns were the main source of food for all California tribes. Acorn flour was as important to the California Native Americans as wheat is to us today. Five types of California oak trees produced acorns that could be eaten. Those from black oak and tanbark oak seem to have been the favorite kinds.

Since some acorns tasted better than others, the tastiest ones were collected first. If harvest of the favorite acorn was poor some years, then less tasty acorns had to be eaten all winter long.

So important were acorns to California Indians that most tribes built their entire year around them. Acorn harvest marked the beginning of their calendar year. Winter was counted as so many months after acorn harvest, and summer was counted by the number of months before the next acorn harvest.

Acorn harvest ceremonies usually were the biggest events of the year. Most celebrations took place in mid-October and included dancing, feasts, games of chance, and reunions with relatives. Harvest festivals lasted for many days. They were a time of joy for everyone.

The annual acorn gathering lasted two to three weeks. Young boys climbed the oak trees to shake branches; some men used long poles to knock acorns to the ground. Women loaded the nuts into large cone-shaped burden baskets and carried them to a central place where they were put in the sun to dry.

Once the acorns were dried, the women carried them back to the tribe's permanent villages. There they lined special basket-like storage granaries with strong herbs to keep insects away, then stored the acorns inside. Granaries were placed on stilts to keep animals from getting into them and were kept beside tribal houses.

Preparing acorns for each meal was also the women's job. Shells were peeled by hitting the acorns with a stone hammer on an anvil (flat) stone. Meat from the nut was then laid on a stone mortar. A mortar was usually a large stone with a slight dip on its surface. Sometimes the mortar had a bottomless basket, called a hopper, glued to its top. This kept the acorn meat from sliding off the mortar as it was beaten. The meat was then pounded with a long stone pestle. Acorn flour was scraped away from the hopper's sides with a soaproot fiber brush during this process.

From there the flour was put into an open-worked basket and sifted. A fine flour came through the bottom of the basket, while the larger pieces were put back in the mortar for more pounding.

The most important process came after the acorn flour was sifted. Acorn flour has a very bitter-tasting tannin in it. This bitter taste was removed by a method called leaching. Many tribes leached the flour by first scooping out a hollow in sand near water. The hollow was lined with leaves to keep the flour from washing away. A great deal of hot water was poured through the flour to wash out (leach) the bitterness. Sometimes the flour was put into a basket for the leaching process, instead of using sand and leaves.

Finally the acorn flour was ready to be cooked. To make mush, heated stones were placed in the basket with the flour. A looped tree branch or two long sticks were used to toss the hot rocks around so the basket would not burn. When the mush had boiled, it could be eaten. If the flour and water mixture was baked in an earthen oven, it became a kind of bread. Early explorers wrote that it was very tasty.

Historians have estimated that one family would eat from 1500 to 2000 pounds of acorn flour a year. One reason California native Americans did not have to plant seeds and raise crops was because there were so many acorns for them to harvest each year.

Whether they ate fish or shellfish or plant food or animal meat, nature supplied more than enough food for the Native Americans who lived in California long ago. Many believed their good fortune in having fine weather and plenty to eat came from being good to their gods.

RELIGION

Tribal members had strong beliefs in the power of spirits or gods around them. Each tribe was different, but all felt the importance of never making a spirit angry with them. For that reason a celebration to thank the spirit-gods for treating them well, took place before each food gathering and before each hunting trip, and after each food harvest.

Usually spiritual powers were thought to belong to birds or animals. Most California tribespeople felt bears were very wicked and should not be eaten. But Coyote seems to have been a kind leader who helped them if they were in trouble, even though he seems to have been a bit naughty at times. Eagle was thought to be very powerful and good to native Americans. In some tribes, Eagle was almost as powerful as Sun.

Tribes placed importance on different gods, according to the tribe's needs. Rain gods were the most important spirits to desert tribes. Weather gods, who might bring less rain or warmer temperatures, were important to northern tribes. A great many groups felt there were gods for each of the winds: North, South, East and West. The four directions were usually included in their ceremonial dances and were used as part of the decorations on baskets, pots, and even tools.

Animals were not only worshipped and believed to be spirit-gods, like Deer or Antelope, but tribal members felt there was a personal animal guardian for each one of them. If a tribal member had a deer as guardian, then that person could never kill a deer or eat deer meat.

California Native Americans believed in life after death. This made them very respectful of death and very fearful of angering a dead person. Once someone died, the name of the dead person could never again be said aloud. Since it was easy to accidentally say a name aloud, the name was usually given to a new baby. Then the dead person would not become angry.

Shamans were thought to be the keepers of religious beliefs and to have the ability to talk directly to spirit-gods. It was the job of a village shaman to cure sick people, and to speak to the gods about the needs of the people. Some tribes had several kinds of shamans in one village. One shaman did curing, one scared off evil spirits, while another took care of hunters.

Not all shamans were nice, so people greatly feared their power. However, if shamans had no luck curing sick people or did not bring good luck in hunting, the people could kill them. Most shamans were men, but in a few tribes, women were doctors.

Most California tribal myths have been lost to history because they were spoken and never written down. The legends were told and retold on winter nights around the home fires. Sadly, these were forgotten after the missionaries brought Christianity to California and moved tribal members into the missions.

A few stories still remain, however. It is thought by historians that northwest California tribes were the only ones not to have a myth on how they were created. They did not feel that the world was made and prepared for human beings. Instead, their few remaining stories usually tell of mountain peaks or rivers in their own territory.

The central California tribes had creation stories of a great flood where there was only water on earth. They tell of how man was made from a bit of mud that a turtle brought up from the bottom of the water.

Many southwest tribes believed there was a time of no sky or water. They told of two clouds appearing which finally became Sky and Earth.

Throughout California, however, all tribes had myths that told of Eagle as the leader, Coyote as chief assistant, and of less powerful spirits like Falcon or Hawk.

Costumes for religious ceremonies often imitated these animals they worshipped or feared. Much time was spent in making the dance costumes as beautiful as possible. Red woodpecker feathers were so brilliant a color they were used to decorate religious headdresses, necklaces, or belts. Deerskin clothing was fringed so shell beads could be attached to each thin strip of leather.

Eagle feathers were felt to be the most sacred of religious objects. Sometimes they were made into whole robes.

Religious feather charm.

Usually, though, the feathers were used just for decorations. All these costumes were valuable to the people of each tribe. The village chief was in charge of taking care of the costumes, and there was terrible punishment for stealing them. Clothing worn everyday was not fancy like costuming for rituals.

Willow bark skirt.

CLOTHING

Central and southern California's fine weather made regular clothes not really very important to the Native Americans. The children and men went naked most of the year, but most women wore a short apron-like skirt. These skirts were usually made in two pieces, front and back aprons, with fringes cut into the bottom edges. Often the skirt was made from the inner bark of trees, shredded and gathered on a cord. Sometimes the skirt was made from tule or grass.

In northern California and in rainy or windy weather elsewhere in the state, animal-skin blankets were worn by both men and women. They were used like a cape and wrapped around the body. Sometimes the cape was put over one shoulder and under the other arm, then tied in front. All kinds of skins were used; deer, otter, wildcat, but sea-otter fur was thought to be the best. If the skin was from a small animal, it was cut into strips and woven together into a fabric. At night the cape became a blanket to keep the person warm.

Because of the rainy weather in northern California, the women wore basket caps all the time. Women of the central and south tribes wore caps only when carrying heavy loads, where the forehead had to be used as support. Then a cap helped keep too much weight from being placed on the forehead.

Most California people went barefoot in their villages. For journeys into rough land, going to war, wood gathering, or in colder weather, the tribesmen in central and northwest California wore a one-piece soft shoe with no extra sole, which went high up on the leg.

Southern California tribespeople, however, wore sandals most of the time, wearing high, soled moccasins only when they traveled long distances or into the mountains. Leggings of skin were worn in snow, and moccasins were sometimes lined with grass for more comfort and warmth.

VILLAGE LIFE

Houses of the California tribes were made of materials found in their area. Usually they were round with domed roofs. Except for a few tribes, a house floor was dug into the earth a few feet. This was wise, for it made the home warmer in winter and cooler in summer. It also meant that less material was needed to make house walls.

Framework for the walls was made from bendable branches tied to support poles. Some frames of the houses were covered with earth and grass. Others were covered with large slabs of redwood or pine bark. Central California

Split-stick clapper, rhythm instrument. Hupa tribe.

villagers made large woven mats of tule reed to cover the tops and sides of houses. In the warmer southern area, brush and smaller pieces of bark were used for house walls.

Most California Native American villages had a building called a sweathouse, where the men could be found when they were not hunting, fishing or traveling. It was a very important place for the men, who used it rather like a clubhouse. They could sweat and then scrape themselves clean with curved ribs of deer. The sweathouse was smaller than a family house. Normally it had a center pole framework with a firepit on the ground next to the pole. When the fire was lit, some smoke was allowed to escape through a hole at the top of the roof; however, most was trapped inside the building. Smoke and heat were the main reasons for having a sweathouse. Both were believed to be a way to purify tribal members' bodies. Sweathouse walls were mainly hard-packed earth. The heat produced was not a steam heat but came from a wood-fed fire.

In the center of most villages was a large house that often had no walls, just a roof held up with poles. It was here that religious dances and rituals were held, or visitors were entertained.

Dances were enjoyed and were performed with great skill. Music, usually only rhythm instruments, accompanied the dances. For some reason California Native Americans did not use drums to create rhythms for their dances. Three different kinds of rattles were used by California tribes.

One type, split-clap sticks, created rhythm for dancing. These were usually a length of cane (a hollow stick) split in half lengthwise for about two-thirds of its length. The part still uncut was tightly wound with cord so it would not split all the way. The stick was held at the tied end in one hand and hit against the palm of the other hand to make its sound.

A pebble-filled moth cocoon made rhythm for shaman duties. These could range from calling on spirits to cure illnesses, to performing dances to bring rain. Probably the best sounds to beat rhythm for songs and dances came from bundles of deer hooves tied together on a stick. These rattles have a hollow, warm sound.

The only really "musical" instrument found in California was a flute made of reed that was played by blowing across the edge of one end. Melodies were not played on any of these instruments. Most North American Indians sang their songs rather than playing melodies on music instruments.

Special songs were sung for each event. There were songs for healing sick people, songs for success in hunting, war, or marriage. Women sang acorn-grinding songs and lullabies. Songs were sung in sorrow for the dead and during storytelling times. Group singing, with a leader, was the favorite kind of singing. Most songs were sung by all tribe members, but religious songs had to be sung by a special group. It was important that sacred songs not be changed through the years. If a mistake was made while singing sacred music, the singer could be punished, so only specially trained singers would sing ritual songs.

All songs were very short, some of them only 20 to 30 seconds long. They were made longer by repeating the melodies over and over, or by connecting several songs together. Songs usually told no story, just repeated words or phrases or syllables in patterns.

Song melodies used only one or two notes and harmony was never added. Perhaps that is why mission Indians, at those missions with musician priests, especially loved to sing harmony in the church choirs.

Songs and dances were good methods of passing rich tribal traditions on to the children. It was important to tribal adults that their children understand and love the tribe's heritage.

Children were truly wanted by parents in most tribes and new parents carefully watched their tiny babies day and night, to be sure they stayed warm and dry. Usually a newborn was strapped into a cradle and tied to the mother's back so she could continue to work, yet be near the baby at all times. In some tribes, older children took care of babies of cradle age during the day to give the mother time to do all her work, while grandmothers were often in charge of caring for toddlers.

Children were taught good behavior, traditions, and tribal rules from babyhood, although some tribes were stricter than others. Most of the time parents made their children obey. Young children could be lightly punished, but in many tribes those over six or seven years old were more severely punished if they did not follow the rules.

Just as children do today, Native American youngsters had childhood traditions they followed. For instance, one tribal tradition said that when a baby tooth came out, a child waited until dusk, faced the setting sun and threw the tooth to the west. There is no mention of a generous tooth fairy, however.

Tribal parents were worried that their offspring might not be strong and brave. Some tribes felt one way to make their children stronger was by forcing them to bathe in ice cold water, even in wintertime. Every once in a while, for example, Modoc children were awakened from sleep and taken to a cold lake or stream for a freezing bath.

But if freezing baths at night were hard on young Native Americans, their days were carefree and happy. Children were allowed to play all day, and some tribes felt children did not even have to come to dinner if they didn't want to. In those tribes, children could come to their houses to eat anytime of the day.

The games boys played are not too different from those played today. Swimming, hide and seek among the tule reeds, a form of tetherball with a mud ball tied to a pole, and willow-javelin throwing kept boys busy throughout the day.

Fathers made their sons small bows and arrows, so boys spent much time trying to improve their hunting skills. They practised shooting at frogs or chipmunks. The first animal any boy killed was not touched or eaten by him. Others would carry the kill home to be cooked and eaten by villagers. This tradition taught boys always to share food.

Another hunting tool for boys was a hollowed-out willow branch. This became like a modern day beanshooter, only the Native American boys shot juniper berries instead of beans. Slingshots made good hunting weapons, as well.

Girls and boys shared many games, but girls playing with each other had contests to see who could make a basket the fastest, or they played with dolls made of tule. Together, young boys and girls played a type of ring-around-the-rosie game, climbed mountains, or built mud houses.

As children grew older, the boys followed their fathers and the girls followed their mothers as the adults did their daily work. Children were not trained in the arts of hunting or basketmaking, however, until they became teenagers.

HISTORY

Spanish missionaries, led by Fray Junipero Serra, arrived in California in 1769 to build missions along the coast of California. By 1823, fifty years later, 21 missions had been founded. Almost all of them were very successful, and the Franciscan monks who ran them were proud of how many Native Americans became Christians.

However, all was not as the monks had planned it would be. Native American people had never been around the diseases European white men brought with them. As a result, they had no immunity to such illnesses as measles, small pox, or flu. Too many mission Indians died from white men's diseases.

Historians figure there were 300,000 Native Americans living in California before the missionaries came. The missions show records of 83,000 mission Indians during mission days. By the time the Mexicans took over the missions from the Spanish in 1834, only 20,000 remained alive.

The great California Gold Rush of 1849 was probably another big reason why many of the Native Americans died during that time. White men, staking their claim to tribal lands with gold upon it, thought nothing of killing any California tribesman who tried to keep and protect his territory. Fifty-thousand tribal members died from diseases, bullets, or starvation between the gold Rush Days and 1870. By 1910, only 17,000 California Indians remained.

Although the American government tried to set aside reservations (areas reserved for Native Americans), the land given to the Indians often was not good land. Worse yet, some of the land sacred to tribes, such as burial grounds, was taken over by white people and never given back.

Sadly, mission Indians, when they became Christians, forgot the proud heritage and beliefs they had followed for thousands of years. Many wonderful myths and songs they had passed from one generation to the next, on winter nights so long ago, have been lost forever.

Today some 100,000 people can claim California Native American ancestors, but few pure-blooded tribespeople remain. Our link with the Wanderers, who came from Asia so long ago, has been forever broken.

The bullroarer made a deep, loud sound when whirled above the player's head. Tipai tribe.

Villages were usually built beside a lake, stream, or river. Balsa canoes are on the shore. Tule reeds grow along the edge of the water and are drying on poles on the right side of the picture.

Women preparing food in baskets, sit on tule mats. Tule mats are being tied to the willow pole framework of a house being built by one of the men.

EASTERN MIWOK TRIBE

The Miwok (Mee' walk) people have been divided into three large groups by anthropologists (historians who study the lives of ancient people). They were placed into groups according to the languages they spoke and according to where they lived.

Northernmost of the three groups were the Lake Miwoks. West and south of the Lake Miwoks were the Coast Miwok people. The third group of Miwoks was called Eastern Miwok. Eastern Miwok territory went from the modern city of Walnut Creek, near Mt. Diablo, north to where the city of Sacramento is today, then northeast to the foothills and higher mountains of the Sierra Mountain range.

This section of Miwok people had several tribelets within it, and each tribelet thought of itself as a separate and independent nation. A tribelet had several permanent villages and an even larger number of food-gathering campsites. Villagers visited different campsites in the spring, summer, or autumn of every year.

Nuts, seeds, or plants were collected at some campsites. Other sites provided large animals for them to hunt, or fish for them to catch. Tribal members always had to gather not just enough food for their needs that day, but food which they would store to take care of their families during the coming winter months.

The population of a tribelet ranged from 100 people to as many as 500. Each tribelet owned territory with well-marked boundaries. Everything inside the boundaries, from plants and animals to minerals, belonged to the tribelet.

THE VILLAGE

Permanent settlements, or villages, could have as few as twenty-five people living in them but usually the villages were larger. Most villages in a tribelet were fairly close together. Several generations of one family lived in a village, so that everyone was related to someone else.

Four kinds of buildings were found in a village. Houses were of different styles, (depending upon where they were found in the territory.) In mountain areas, the main home was cone-shaped and made of three or four layers of bark slabs taken from trees growing there.

In the valleys, a house was also cone-shaped but had poles for framework. Thatches of grass and brush were placed on top of the framework. This kind of house also was built at food-gathering sites in the mountains during summer months.

Another kind of permanent house was cone-shaped and had woven tule mats laid over the framework. It was found in the lower foothill area of the Sierra Mountains.

The fourth kind of house was built only by richer tribal members in the northeast plains of the territory. This house had a floor dug into the earth about the depth of a foot or two. A framework of poles was first covered in thatch and then with dirt, making the house look like a large mound of earth. Cold winds did not enter this house as they would the smaller above-ground homes.

A fire pit was usually in the center of all houses, and some of the cooking was done there. An earth oven, a small rounded

Roundhouse.

mound of packed dirt shaped like a beehive, was found near the fire pit. Meals were usually prepared and cooked outside during good weather.

Dirt floors were covered with digger, or yellow, pine needles. Often woven tule mats and deerskin covered the pine needles on the floor. These mats and deerskins also made excellent blankets for those villagers who slept on the floor at night. Chiefs, or other important village men, had beds made of poles with bearskins attached to them.

Two different kinds of assembly houses might be found in a settlement. One type was a large round building dug into the earth as deep as three or four feet. This kind of ceremonial house was found in permanent villages and was the center for most religious and social events.

These permanent assembly houses were from 40 to 50 feet long, and had a roof held up by four tall center poles. The support poles caused the roof to have a shape rather like that of a long circus tent, the bottom of which rested on the edge of the circular hole dug for the floor.

Cross sticks were laid on the support poles and brush was laid on top of the cross sticks. A layer of yellow pine needles covered the brush. Finally, soil was placed over the whole roof. A door was made at the bottom of the large mound by digging into the earth.

A second kind of assembly house was built in food-gathering sites, where a village lived while gathering food. It was mainly used for funerals, in case a tribal member died while the villagers were away from their permanent home. This kind of assembly house was not as large or grand as those built in the permanent village. It was usually roofed in brush, or pine needles covered with brush; the walls were thin enough to let in any cooling summer breezes.

Each permanent village had a sweathouse. Most were from six to fifteen feet in diameter, round, and built over a pit two to three feet deep. The sweathouse was also cone-shaped and covered with layers of pine needles, brush, and earth.

A sweathouse was used for curing diseases, for steam purification of hunters before hunting trips, and was the social center for men during the days they were at home in the village. Hunting and fishing weapons and tools were repaired at the sweathouse. Fishing nets were made or repaired here. The building was used almost like a modern men's club.

One interesting building mentioned in the history of this tribe was a small grinding hut. It was a mound-shaped hut built over a large flat rock. The purpose of the building was to give women some protection from the weather as they ground grains and seeds. The large rock made an excellent mortar and the grinding hut allowed daily grinding to go on at any time of the year.

Every village had several granaries which stored the nuts and grains villagers had gathered in the fall. Granaries were built in the shape of today's paper towel rolls, only much larger, of course. Some granaries were twelve feet tall and five feet in diameter (across).

The walls of a granary were built with a framework of tall poles. Grapevines were wound around both the tall poles and smaller poles, which were put in between. Inside, the walls were lined with grass. The bottom of a granary was made of a layer of twigs and brush. Granaries helped the villagers protect their acorn supply from animals and birds.

Yosemite Miwok acorn granary.

VILLAGE LIFE

Tribelet chiefs were the leaders of settlements, or villages. The office of chief was inherited from a father or mother. Most chiefs were men, but if a chief who died had no son, then his daughter became leader. Sometimes a chief died before a son was old enough to take on the job. When that happened the widow of the chief would rule until the child was old enough to lead the people of the tribelet.

A chief had the duty of settling arguments between villagers and was expected to order criminals put to death, if necessary. Chiefs were also the tribelets' war leaders but did not actually take part in battles themselves. Wars very often came about when people of other tribelets trespassed on a tribelet's territory to gather food. Tribelets also went to war when unfriendly tribes raided one of their villages.

Chiefs decided when to have public ceremonies or feasts. A chief furnished all the food for such an event. Although chiefs did no hunting for their families, they had several young, single men who hunted for them. In return for their hunting, the young hunters were fed by the chief's family.

The family of a chief wore special clothing. They wore buckskin belts with decorations of beautiful woodpecker scalps and olivella disk beads, for example. Such beautiful clothing was very valuable and showed the wealth of the chief and his family.

Assistants to a chief had the titles of speakers and messengers. They were considered important tribal members. It was a speaker's duty to make announcements from the roof of the assembly house each day. Some days the announcements from the chief, delivered by the speaker, were about good behavior or preparing food. Other days the message might be of the need to go on gathering trips.

Speakers also had the jobs of finding food gifts and religious items for ceremonies and passing out food during ceremonies. Speakers were elected to their jobs by villagers.

Messengers were in charge of taking all ceremonial invitations to neighboring tribelets. Another duty was to act as announcer at ritual and ceremonial events. Like the speaker, a messenger announced from the roof of the assembly house. The office of messenger was a hereditary one, inherited from father to son.

Other important tribelet people included the hunters and fishermen who supplied the chief's family with food, four ceremonial cooks who prepared food for ceremonies and religious rituals, and the fire tender of the assembly house.

RELIGION AND BELIEFS

The Miwoks believed all living things on this earth belonged to either Land or Water. Animals were chosen by families to represent them as being either on the Water side or the Land side of these two halves of the world.

Invitation string.

For instance, people of the Central Sierra tribelet used a bluejay to represent those families belonging to Land and the frog as representing those families belonging to Water. Giving families different names made it easier to remember the ones who were closely related and those who were not.

Even the personal names of the people reflected how they were related to an animal or fish family. Names of those in the Water group included words like salmon or water, while members of the Land group might have used words like bear or rabbit in their names.

The presence of families from both the Land and Water groups was needed in ceremonies throughout the year. In funeral ceremonies, the group different from a dead person's family was in charge of preparing the body for burial. During a girl's teenage ceremony, girls from the two different groups exchanged dresses with each other.

Myths handed down from generation to generation were also about animals, birds, or fish. The most important animals in Eastern Miwok myths were Coyote, Prairie Falcon, and Condor. Eastern Miwoks believed Condor was the father of Prairie Falcon. Coyote was Condor's father and Prairie Falcon's grandfather. Many myths were about how Coyote and Prairie Falcon won battles with monsters they said had once lived on Miwok land.

Religion in the Eastern Miwok tribe was the responsibility of village shamans. These spirit doctors were supposed to be able to speak to spirit-gods more easily than regular villagers. Shamans inherited their positions from their fathers. Each shaman had his own area of power, which came to him in dreams or through trances.

One kind of shaman was thought to be able to remove diseases from an ill person's body. It was his job to locate the disease first, then to decide the symbol for the disease so it could be removed. This kind of shaman was actually like our modern-day magician. He used sleight-of-hand tricks to appear to remove a feather, rock, or any object thought to be the disease symbol, from the body of the sick tribal member.

Herbal shamans gave out medicine made from plants to cure sicknesses which were not serious. Many of the plant medicines a curing doctor used in ancient days are still used by modern doctors today.

Some shamans, called deer doctors, were thought to be able to look into the future and tell how successful a deer hunt would be. They were also supposed to be able to locate where deer could be found. Rattlesnake shamans handled rattlesnakes at ceremonies.

Weather shamans claimed they had control over weather. It was believed these weather doctors could cause rain and wind to start or stop. Bear shamans, who were supposed to have bears as their spirit guardians, often danced at religious ceremonies.

Eastern Miwoks had two kinds of ceremonies. Sacred religious events included dances which had to be performed exactly the right way, with the belief that dancers making mistakes might suffer from a terrible illness. Dancers wore very fancy costumes at these religious ceremonies.

The second kind of ceremony was held just to entertain tribal members and visitors. No punishment could come from making a mistake while dancing at this kind of event, nor were highly decorated costumes worn at these nonreligious ceremonies.

CLOTHING

Unlike ritual dance costumes, everyday clothing was not fancy. Children wore no clothes at all. Women in the northern mountain area wore a one-piece, wrap-around dress of deerskin. In the central part of Eastern Miwok territory, the women wore a two-piece skirt of deerskin or grass. Plains women wore the same style of skirts as those of the central tribelets, but the plains women had skirts made of shredded tule fabric. A skirt was made of two aprons, one in front and one in back.

Eastern Miwok men wore buckskin loincloths. In cold weather, both men and women wore robes of prepared skins, using the

Bighead dance costume.

hides of deer, bear, mountain lion, coyote, or buffalo. Sometimes tribal members wore blankets made of woven rabbit-skin strips with feathers woven into the strips.

Hair was worn long and was cut off only when a close relative died, as a sign of mourning. Soaproot fiber brushes were used to keep the hair tidy. Hair was washed every few days with lather from the soaproot plant.

Some tribal members let their hair flow loosely; others held theirs away from the face with a headband of beaver skin or string. Often a feather rope tied hair into a pony tail at the back of the neck. Once in a while, on special occasions, regular villagers wore hair nets. Chiefs wore hairnets every day.

Tattooing, worn by both men and women, usually was done in straight lines from chin to navel. Body paints were put on for ceremonies. Dye colors were red, white, and black.

Soaproot brush.

Red dye came from a mineral the Eastern Miwoks got in trade from the East Mono tribe. White color came from using chalk. Black was always easy to get; it came from charcoal found in their own fires.

Children had their ear lobes and noses pierced while they were still quite young. Both boys and girls wore flowers in their ears. Women wore earrings of beads and shells. Men wore ear plugs of bird bone with a white feather added. Men also wore nose sticks which were either polished bone or shell.

Skins used for clothing were prepared by the men. A deer hide was staked out on the ground, scraped with sharp rock flakes, and allowed to dry for a few days. The hide was then soaked in water for a few more days. Next, the skin was soaked overnight in a solution of deer brains. This was followed by stretching and pulling the skin until it was soft. Last, sharp-edged deer-bone scrapers were used to remove all hair from the hide.

Obsidian hide scraper.

Bear hides were covered with rotting wood to soak up most of the fat. A wooden tool was used to scrape off all extra flesh. Bear skins were not softened but allowed to stay stiff and hard.

Only the Plains tribelet of the Eastern Miwoks used tule for clothing fabric. The tribelet's main uses of tule, however, were for woven mats used as floor covering, and for balsa boats. String and rope were made from milkweed-stalk fiber or Indian-hemp fiber. Milkweed fiber for string was removed from the plant by placing bundles of the stalk on a man's thigh and rolling them downward with the right hand until only the inside strings were left. These fibers were then braided, or rolled together to make strong cord. Fish nets and net bags, used for storage and carrying, were made from these fibers.

TRADE

Obsidian was a volcanic glass which flaked off into pieces of hard stone with sharp edges. Because of obsidian's sturdy sharp edge, it was wanted by most California tribes for arrowheads and knife blades. Obsidian was found in the mountain territories of the Mono and Washo tribes. Traders of these tribes offered obsidian, plus salt, to their neighbors, the Sierra tribelet of the Eastern Miwoks. The Sierra tribelet, in turn, traded the obsidian and salt they did not use to the Plains tribelet of their own tribe. The Plains tribelet then exchanged the obsidian and salt with Ohlones for Olivella and haliotis shells, which could be used for decoration or as shell money.

The Valley tribelet of the Eastern Miwoks traded for bows made by tribes in the western coastal mountain range and in the eastern Sierra mountains. There were many trees growing in mountain areas which had excellent wood for bows. Baskets were also traded among the tribes and tribelets.

Trading was a way to get most things a village needed. Trading was also a way to keep ideas moving between tribes. Methods of making baskets were shared this way. The women of some tribes were better basketmakers than those of other tribes. When one of these excellent baskets was traded to a tribe which had not seen that kind before, the basket was copied by the women. Sometimes they even improved on the pattern of the original basket. In this way, ideas and improvements could pass from one tribe to another.

BASKETS

Eastern Miwok tribal women made both twined and coiled baskets. Usually willow branches were used for twined baskets. Seed beaters, the large burden baskets carried on women's backs, open-weave baskets for sifting flour, and unusual winnowing baskets shaped like a triangle, were all twined.

Seed beaters had a handle attached so the women could collect grass seeds in them by swishing them through tall grass and hitting the seed grain into the round shallow basket. A winnowing basket was like a flat tray and was used to throw grains into the air, causing the outer coating to blow away in the wind and the heavier grain to fall back into the tray. Baby cradles and rackets for ball games were twined as well.

This tribe thought a flattened head was beautiful, so their baby cradles were made without padding in order to flatten the back of a baby's head on the hard wood of the cradle. The forehead of a baby was rubbed and pressed from the center

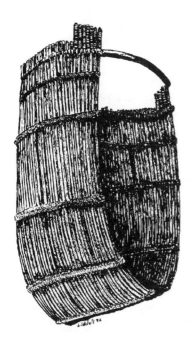

to the sides of the head to flatten the forehead. Some parents even liked the look of flattened noses.

Coiled baskets were much stronger, since coils of two or three slender branches were wound together with a strong fiber. Coiled baskets were so tightly woven, they were used as cooking and parching baskets.

FOOD

Tribal women were in charge of gathering wild plants and preparing all foods. There were many seed-bearing plants growing in Eastern Miwok territory. Not only did the plants provide summer food for tribal members, they drew many large animals, like deer, antelope, and elk to tribal territory to graze. This made hunting to get meat for winter food a far easier job for tribal hunters.

To make sure there was always a good supply of plants, each August villagers burned fields and the ground under forest trees. Eastern Miwoks knew that plants produce more seeds the year after being burned.

Seeds were gathered in May through August of every year and were the main foods eaten during those months. Wild oats, seeds from flowering evening primrose, redmaids, California buttercup, and ripgut grass, were the favorites.

Greens were usually gathered in the early spring and eaten with bread or mush made from acorn flour. The flour was made, when needed, from acorns which had been stored in granaries the past autumn. Columbine, milkweed, wild pea, and twiggy water dropwort were just a few of the greens tribal members enjoyed.

Roots of several wild plants made potato-like food for villagers. Roots were dug up by village women, who used strong digging sticks to remove them from the ground. The kinds of roots found in Eastern Miwok land included squawroot and corn lily. Although wild berries were an important summer food for most inland tribes, the Eastern Miwoks found only a few growing on their land.

There were many kinds of nuts in tribal territory, however, which only needed to be gathered in the fall of the year. Hazelnuts, digger pine nuts, and sugar pine nuts were popular with the tribelets. Digger pine nuts could be eaten green in the spring, and eaten ripe in the autumn.

The most important nut was the acorn. Seven kinds of oak trees grew on tribal land but the acorns from some trees were tastier than others. The Plains tribelets of the Eastern Miwoks liked acorns from valley oak trees best. Foothill tribelets enjoyed the acorns from the blue oak and live oak trees. Mountain tribelets preferred black oak acorns.

Acorns were usually allowed to ripen and fall to the ground by themselves, but sometimes sticks were used to knock them off the branches. The acorns were placed in large cone-shaped burden baskets and hauled back to the permanent village on women's backs. Turn back to chapter one of this book to review how acorns were prepared.

Animal foods were mostly eaten in the winter months, when bodies needed more energy to keep warm. Mule deer meat was the most important meat to foothill and mountain tribelets. Tule elk and pronghorn antelope were the main meats eaten by Plains tribelets.

Foothill tribelets also ate grizzly bears and black bears. Smaller animals, like black-tailed jackrabbits and cottontails, were eaten. Beaver, gray squirrels, and woodrats made good food, also. The most important birds eaten were valley quail and mountain quail. Plains tribelets caught waterfowl, like duck and geese, for many of their meals.

Villagers moved about, throughout the year, leaving their permanent village to travel from valleys to mountains as plant food ripened. The highest land was visited in hot summer months, when village hunters followed deer. Sometimes the Foothills tribelets went to the Central Valley to hunt antelope and tule elk.

Salmon was the major kind of fish eaten by the Plains villagers. Trout were caught in mountain streams, and lamprey eels were eaten by all Eastern Miwoks.

All tribal members found grasshoppers and the eggs of yellow jackets particularly tasty. Eastern Miwoks did not eat coyotes, skunks, eagles, roadrunners, great horned owls, or any snakes or frogs.

Eastern Miwoks were able to store great amounts of acorns because of their large granaries. Granaries were placed near houses in the villages so they could be better protected.

Earth oven.

Most other food was stored in large, flat-bottomed storage baskets and kept inside the houses. Grasshoppers and plant greens were steamed and dried before storing. Quail, deer meat, and fish were dried by the sun or by the heat of fire to preserve them.

Food preparation was the tribal women's job. Baking and steaming was done in an earth oven. Roots, greens, and grasshoppers were also baked in the oven. Meat from large animals was usually cut in strips and broiled over a fire. Birds, fish, and small animals were roasted whole in the ashes of a fire.

Seeds were mostly eaten as pinole, flour made from ground-up seeds. Pinole was made by first winnowing seeds in a basket. The husked seeds were then cooked by tossing them with live coals in a basket tray. This method of cooking is called parching. The cooked seeds were then ground into a flour with a mortar and pestle. Pinole was either eaten dry or made into a delicious mush, which was eaten with the fingers.

Acorn soup was made by boiling the acorn meal in baskets. Boiling was done by placing hot rocks in with meal and water. Water, meal, and stones were then stirred with a wooden paddle until the meal was cooked. As the rocks cooled, they were removed from the basket and placed in a basket of water to be rinsed. Some acorn bread was baked in earth ovens. Other tribelets made bread by putting the meal on a hot stone and turning it as it cooked.

HUNTING AND FISHING

Usually deer were hunted by a group of hunters who surrounded an area, driving the trapped deer off a cliff or into a net. Sometimes hunters encircled the deer with small fires to keep them trapped until they could be killed.

When a single hunter went after deer, he wore a deer head on his own head as a disguise. The deer head allowed a hunter to get close enough to a deer so it could be more easily shot with arrows. Single hunters often chased a deer until it was too tired to run any longer. Deer were most frequently found near trails they made to watering holes, or when they were grazing in fields.

Yokut arrow made with a cane shaft. Obsidian arrow point is attached to the front shaft, which sets into the larger back shaft at A. Fletching at the back end of the shaft is of clipped feathers.

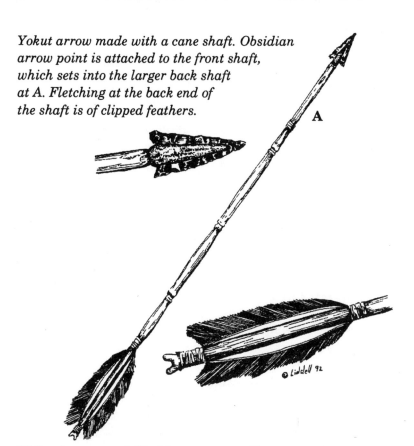

If the deer were killed by a group of hunters, the meat was evenly divided among them. If a single hunter killed a deer, he shared it among his relatives. The more distant relatives were given what was left of the animal after the close relatives took the legs.

Groups of 12, or more, hunters went after bears. Rabbits were often caught by a whole village working together. Villagers chased rabbits into nets sometimes three or four feet high and 1,200 feet long!

Bows and arrows were the major hunting weapons. They were also needed for fighting wars. Eastern Miwok bows were usually made of cedar, but other woods for making bows might have been ash, oak, willow, pepperwood, or hazel. Several layers of animal tendons (called sinew) were attached to the back of a bow with glue made from the root

41

of the soaproot plant. Sinew made the bow much more flexible, allowing the arrows to fly greater distances.

Tribal hunters had many different kinds of arrows. For war and hunting large animals, a hunting arrow was best. The front part of the arrow shaft was designed to stay in the enemy, or animal, even if the rest of the shaft was removed. Ordinary hunting arrows were made with the stone arrowhead attached to a single, main arrow shaft. Arrows without stone points were used in hunting small game, fish, and birds. Those arrows were simply hardened by fire and sharpened to a point. Arrows usually had a fletching pattern of three feathers at the back end, which kept the direction of the arrow straight. Most of the feathers used for fletching were red-tailed hawk feathers.

Tools used in making bows included an obsidian flake and a scraper made from the leg bone of a deer. These tools were used to shape the bow. Fine sanding of bows and arrows was done with rough stones or pieces of scratchy cane stalk.

There were two types of arrow straighteners: one of wood or stone, and another made from steatite (soapstone). In both types of straighteners, a long, straight groove was cut into the wood or stone. An arrow shaft was soaked in water, then laid in the groove to dry. Straight arrows meant more accurate shots by hunters. Arrowheads were held on a buckskin pad while deer-antler points chipped and shaped the obsidian or flint stone into its proper shape.

There were two kinds of quivers used for holding arrows. The storage quiver was usually a buckskin bag, and it was always left in the hunter's home. On hunting trips, a hunter carried a quiver made of fox or otter skin. This quiver was open at both ends, so an arrow could be easily removed from either end. If a spear was needed, it was usually made from wood of the mountain mahogany tree. A spear was tipped with obsidian because it was the strongest of the flaking stone.

Snares and traps were used to catch smaller animals. A snare with an acorn for bait caught many birds. Woodpeckers' bright red top feathers were needed for the colorful dance costumes. Woodpeckers were caught by plugging up most of their holes in trees, then watching the few remaining holes until a bird appeared. Ducks and geese were caught in nets, either as they ate, or by throwing the netting in front of a bird as it started to fly.

Nets were valuable in fishing, too. Dip nets were used in deep water holes of a river. Dip nets had handles, so they could be used from the shore or from a boat. Seine nets were large, with sinkers on the bottom edge to keep the net hanging vertically. Fishermen made the net into a circle. The top of this kind of net was pulled together with a drawstring to capture fish. The pulled-together net was then hauled ashore to remove the captured fish. This type of net was best in large rivers, especially where water movement was rather slow.

Steatite arrow straightener.

Fishermen sometimes used a spear with an obsidian-tipped point. Spears were thrown from the shore or from a boat. If a boat was used, it probably was a balsa boat made of tightly tied bundles of tule. Sometimes as many as 20 bundles were tied to make a boat. Two willow poles kept the bundles rigid, or stiff, at the sides of the boat, and about eight willow branches were put on the outsides of the bundles, crosswise. A balsa boat was moved with one or two wooden paddles.

In mountain areas, the only kind of boat was really a two-log raft, with the logs tied together. It was needed only to cross streams.

HISTORY

The Eastern Miwok tribe first saw white people when Spanish explorers arrived in the late 1700s. The Spanish had sent Father Junípero Serra to the California area to start missions along the coast. After Coastal tribes became mission Indians, the missionaries began to search for members of inland tribes. In 1794, the Coastal Miwoks became mission Indians at Mission San Francisco (also known as Mission Dolores).

They were followed by the Plains tribelet of the Eastern Miwok tribe, who joined Indians at Mission San José in 1811. Native Americans had never been around white people's illnesses, however, and when they came in contact with measles, smallpox, and flu, their bodies had no immunity to fight such diseases. Tens of thousands of tribal members died from these epidemics.

Most Plains tribelet members were not at all eager to become a part of mission life. Many Eastern Miwok warriors went to war to keep from joining the mission churches. Warriors raided missions on a regular basis. This caused a great deal of anger to build up in the Spanish soldiers, who had been sent to protect the missions. Soldiers would follow runaway Miwoks back to their old villages, capture and return the Native Americans to the missionaries.

It was not until after the 1820s to 1830s that Miwok tribelets finally began to join the missions. By this time, white American settlers had begun to arrive. Not only did settlers take tribal land, they brought new diseases with them causing more Native Americans to die.

In the late 1840s, gold miners tore through the land searching for gold. They were followed by fur trappers and more settlers. The Mountain tribelets of the Eastern Miwoks fought fiercely for a while to protect their ancient territory but could not hold on to their old way of life; there were just too many white people. Disease had killed so many of the tribe that it grew too weak to carry on the fight.

Miwok couple.

Eventually, members of the Valley tribelet started working as field laborers on the large ranches. Gold miners used the Native Americans as miners but continued to kill many of them without a thought. Over 200 Miwoks were killed by miners from 1847 to 1860.

When California became a territory of the United States, Miwok land was taken over by the federal government. Those tribal members not working on rancheros at that time were sent to government reservations near Fresno. In the late 1800s and early 1900s, Miwoks living near the foothills lived partly by hunting and gathering and partly doing seasonal work on farms and ranches. Gradually they came to depend on money more than on their hunting abilities. Most of them were very poor.

Many members of the Plains and Foothill tribelets who were sent to reservations did not return to Miwok territory. Some tribal members did return to the foothills, as the years passed, however. Today there are many persons of Miwok descent living on their old territory, but there are no pure-blood Miwoks. From a population of 19,500 Miwoks in 1805, the 1951 population count showed only 105 pure-blood Eastern Miwok remaining. Today there are no known fullblood Eastern Miwoks.

OUTLINE
EASTERN MIWOK

I. Introduction
    A. Three large groups of Miwoks
    B. Eastern Miwok territory
    C. Tribelets
        1. Population and territory
    D. Permanent villages
        1. House descriptions
        2. Assembly houses and descriptions
        3. Sweathouse and its uses
        4. Granary description

II. Village life
    A. Chief
        1. How chosen and duties
        2. Speakers and messengers and their jobs

III. Religion and Beliefs
    A. Land and Water groups of families
    B. Myths about Coyote, Prairie Falcon, and Condor
    C. Shamans
        1. Curing doctors
        2. Weather and bear shamans
    D. Sacred and dancing ceremonies

IV. Clothing
    A. Ritual dance costumes
    B. Tribal men's clothing
    C. Tribal women's clothing
    D. Hair styles and care
    E. Tattoos and dyeing of skin
    F. Decorations and ornaments
    G. Treating of animal skins for clothing
    H. Uses of tule for clothing
    I. Making and uses of string and cord

V. Trade
    A. Products traded among tribelets and other tribes
    B. Borrowing of ideas between tribes
VI. Baskets
    A. Twined baskets and uses
    B. Coiled baskets and their uses
VII. Foods
    A. Plants
        1. Kinds of plants eaten
        2. When plants were gathered
        3. Acorns, preparation and gathering
    B. Meat
        1. Large and small animals
        2. Places to hunt through the year
    C. Fish
        1. Kinds of fish eaten
        2. Where fish was caught
    D. Special foods eaten
    E. Food preparation
VIII. Hunting and fishing
    A. Hunting
        1. Deer hunting
        2. Hunting weapons
        3. Snares and traps
    B. Fishing
        1. Nets
        2. Spears
        3. Boats
IX. History
    A. White explorers
    B. Missions
    C. Gold Rush
    D. California as a United States territory
    E. Reservations
    F. Today's population of Eastern Miwoks

GLOSSARY

AWL: a sharp, pointed tool used for making small holes in leather or wood

CEREMONY: a meeting of people to perform formal rituals for a special reason; like an awards ceremony to hand out trophies to those who earned honors

CHERT: rock which can be chipped off, or flaked, into pieces with sharp edges

COILED: a way of weaving baskets which looks like the basket is made of rope coils woven together

DIAMETER: the length of a straight line through the center of a circle

DOWN: soft, fluffy feathers

DROUGHT: a long period of time without water

DWELLING: a building where people live

FLETCHING: attaching feathers to the back end of an arrow to make the arrow travel in a straight line

GILL NET: a flat net hanging vertically in water to catch fish by their heads and gills

GRANARIES: basket-type storehouses for grains and nuts

HERITAGE: something passed down to people from their long-ago relatives

LEACHING: washing away a bitter taste by pouring water through foods like acorn meal

MORTAR: flat surface of wood or stone used for the grinding of grains or herbs with a pestle

PARCHING:	to toast or shrivel with dry heat
PESTLE:	a small stone club used to mash, pound, or grind in a mortar
PINOLE:	flour made from ground corn
INDIAN RESERVATION:	land set aside for Native Americans by the United States government
RITUAL:	a ceremony that is always performed the same way
SEINE NET:	a net which hangs vertically in the water, encircling and trapping fish when it is pulled together
SHAMAN:	tribal religious men or women who use magic to cure illness and speak to spirit-gods
SINEW:	stretchy animal tendons
STEATITE:	a soft stone (soapstone) mined on Catalina Island by the Gabrielino tribe; used for cooking pots and bowls
TABOO:	something a person is forbidden to do
TERRITORY:	land owned by someone or by a group of people
TRADITION:	the handing down of customs, rituals, and belief, by word of mouth or example, from generation to generation
TREE PITCH:	a sticky substance found on evergreen tree bark
TWINING:	a method of weaving baskets by twisting fibers, rather than coiling them around a support fiber

NATIVE AMERICAN WORDS WE KNOW AND USE

PLANTS AND TREES
hickory
pecan
yucca
mesquite
saguaro

ANIMALS
caribou
chipmunk
cougar
jaguar
opossum
moose

STATES
Dakota – friend
Ohio – good river
Minnesota – waters that reflect the sky
Oregon – beautiful water
Nebraska – flat water
Arizona
Texas

FOODS
avocado
hominy
maize (corn)
persimmon
tapioca
succotash

GEOGRAPHY
bayou – marshy body of water
savannah – grassy plain
pasadena – valley

WEATHER
blizzard
Chinook (warm, dry wind)

FURNITURE
hammock

HOUSE
wigwam
wickiup
tepee
igloo

INVENTIONS
toboggan

BOATS
canoe
kayak

OTHER WORDS
caucus – group meeting
mugwump – loner politician
squaw – woman
papoose – baby

CLOTHING
moccasin
parka
mukluk – slipper
poncho

BIBLIOGRAPHY

Baker, Rob. *The Clam "Gardens" of Tomales Bay: New from Native California,* pg. 28, Vol. 6, No. 2, Spring, 1992.

Barrett, S.A. and Gifford, E.W. *Miwok Material Culture.* Yosemite National Park, California: Yosemite Association, 1933.

Cressman, L.S. *Prehistory of the Far West.* Salt Lake City, Utah: University of Utah Press, 1977.

Heizer, Robert F., volume editor. *Handbook of North American Indians, volume 8.* Washington, DC: Smithsonian Institution, 1978.

Heizer, Robert F. and Elsasser, Albert B. *The Natural World of the California Indians.* Berkeley and Los Angeles, CA; London, England: University of California Press, 1980.

Heizer, Robert F. and Whipple, M.A. *The California Indians.* Berkeley and Los Angeles, CA; London, England: University of California Press, 1971.

Heuser, Iva. *California Indians.* PO Box 352, Camino, CA 95709: Sierra Media Systems, 1977.

Macfarlen, Allan and Paulette. *Handbook of American Indian Games.* 31 E. 2nd Street, Mineola, N.Y. 11501: Dover Publications, 1985.

Murphey, Edith Van Allen. *Indian Uses of Native Plants.* 603 W. Perkins Street, Ukiah, CA 95482: Mendocino County Historical Society, copyright renewal, 1987.

National Geographic Society. *The World of American Indians.* Washington, DC: National Geographic Society reprint, 1989

Tunis, Edwin. *Indians.* 2231 West 110th Street, Cleveland, OH: The World Publishing Company, 1959.

Weatherford, Jack. *Native Roots.* 201 E. 50th Street, New York, N.Y.: Crown Publishers, Inc., 1991.

Credits:
Island Industries, Vashon Island, Washington 98070
Dona McAdam, Mac on the Hill, Seattle, Washington 98109

Acknowledgements:
Richard Buchen, Research Librarian, Braun Library, Southwest Museum
Special thanks